This is your daily reminder.

Copyright © 2024 by Lisa Buscomb.

First published 2024

All rights reserved.

This book is copyright. Except for the purpose of fair review, no part may be stored or transmitted in any form or by any means, electronic or mechanical, including recording or storage in any information retrieval system, without permission in writing from the publisher. No reproduction may be made, whether by photocopying or by any other means, unless a licence has been obtained from the publisher

Design & layout by Lisa Buscomb

This is your daily reminder.

Lisa Buscomb

*Here's a gentle reminder
for anyone who might
need it today.*

Welcome to **This Is Your Daily Reminder,** a collection of inspiration and encouragement curated to help you navigate each day with beauty and confidence. For the past year, I've shared seven reminders each week on Instagram that have resonated deeply with so many, encouraging you to know your worth, fall in love with the everyday moments, and trust that you are wildly deserving.

In this book, you'll find a collection of the most loved reminders, alongside many new ones. Each reminder is numbered, allowing you to choose a number before opening the book or to easily remember your favorites. Discover 161 uplifting reminders designed to inspire, support, or reassure. Read them at the start of your day, during quiet moments, or whenever you need a boost. I hope these words bring you comfort and motivation.

As you explore the reminders, take what resonates and leave aside what doesn't connect with you today. Feel free to share them with a friend, maybe they need the reminder at this moment too.

Thank you for allowing me to be a part of your journey. May these reminders inspire you to stay unapologetically you, and celebrate this beautiful life.

With love
Lisa

01

You deserve to be happy.

02

Don't follow every trend. Take what you love,
be inspired, and make it yours.

03

It's time to stop holding yourself back.
You've got this.

04

This week, see challenges as opportunities.

05

The things that other people do,
are not because of you.

06

You are something special.
You are capable, kind and beautiful.

THIS IS YOUR DAILY REMINDER.

Let today be just what it is,
not what you think
it should be.

08

Learn to be spontaneous, to take risks,
to step outside your comfort zone.
Sometimes it's the most beautiful place to be.

09

Be gentle with your thoughts,
they shape your world.

10

In the middle of it all,
remember to take a minute for yourself.

11

When you are okay with not being
everyone's cup of tea;
life becomes so much sweeter.

12

Be proud of how far you have come,
not matter how small the growth may seem.

13

What if I told you that everything meant for you
is on its way,
and all you need to do is believe.

Chasing wild dreams
and making them happen
is what truly makes
life beautiful.

15

Sometimes you don't need an entire village,
you just need one person who really gets you.

16

Take the time to romanticize your life.

17

I believe you should give that thing a go.
What if it turns out even better than you dream of?

18

"you look so happy"
is the most beautiful compliment.

19

What if you believed you could,
instead of thinking you can't?

20

Sometimes, all you need is a long hug
to turn your mood around.

THIS IS YOUR DAILY REMINDER

Give me slow mornings,
the scent of fresh blooms,
coffee in hand,
and sunshine on my skin.

22

Surround yourself with people
who simply, make you feel great.

23

Everything is hard in some moments.
Don't let the hard get you down.
Know that easy will come.

24

You didn't go through all you have for nothing.

25

Believe that the future
has so many beautiful moments.

26

Confidence is found in loving yourself.

27

Your imagination is life's preview
of what's to come.

Where you are heading
is more important
than how long it takes.

29

Treat yourself with kindness and understanding,
especially during challenging times.

30

Curate a curious and open-minded attitude.

31

When you believe that you can,
everything changes.

32

Being outdoors will immediately
change your mood.

33

Always celebrate the small wins.

34

Do something nice for yourself
at least once a day.

THIS IS YOUR DAILY REMINDER

There is such beauty
in the perfectly imperfect.

36

Sometimes you just have to wake up,
sit up and be so incredibly proud
of how far you have come.

37

Just because it's hard
and you are struggling,
doesn't mean that you are failing.

38

Asking for help is a beautiful strength;
it's not a weakness that should make you sad.
It takes courage to reach out when you need to.

39

It's okay to have a bad day.
There are many better days to come.

40

It won't always be easy.
It also won't always be hard either.

41

It's okay if you are missing
the way things used to be.

Do you remember
when you dreamed of
what you have now.

43

There are so many beautiful reasons
to be happy.

44

Start before you have it all figured out.
Nothing has to be perfect
before you take the first step.

45

Be the person you want to be,
not who you think you should be.

46

I hope you give yourself the credit you deserve,
for all that you have achieved this week.

47

Everyone is going through something,
with worrying thoughts
and a heaviness in their heart;
so be gentle & kind.

48

Stay consistent.
Consistency will help you climb the mountain,
no matter how long it takes.

THIS IS YOUR DAILY REMINDER

It's okay to feel excited and nervous,
at the same time.

50

There are so many great things
out there waiting for you.

51

It won't feel this heavy forever.
There is a lightness coming your way very soon.

52

If your life is going to get better,
It's you who will make it happen.

53

Here's to new chapters, new opportunities
and stories unwritten.

54

The world needs the unique magic
that only you hold.

55

Don't take it personally, it's not about you.
It is all about them.

If you close your eyes
and dream about it,
it is worth your time,
energy, and love.

57

Sit up tall, dust yourself off, and try again.

58

I hope you live a life you are proud of,
because the only person you should live to impress
is yourself.

59

There is no right time,
but there is a small opportunity every day
to follow your heart.

60

Just because it's hard
doesn't mean it's impossible.

61

Your future is not defined by your past.

62

You don't need to apologise
for putting yourself first.

THIS IS YOUR DAILY REMINDER

Let go of your fear of failing.
Failure is a step to success.

64

Get up, stretch, get outside, and breathe.
Sometimes nature really is the best medicine.

65

Allow every situation, to be what it is.

66

The best kind of happiness
is happiness you find within.

67

I hope you know it is okay,
to start all over again.

68

Life is a series of struggles;
find comfort within the struggle.

69

When you realise your best is enough,
everything changes.

Be picky about whom
you allow around you.

71

Know that it's okay if not everything works out.

72

Be grateful for your mistakes.
We often learn our greatest lessons
when things don't go quite as expected.

73

Smile someone's way today.
You never know how much
they may need it.

74

It's not your responsibility
to live up to other people's expectations.

75

Not everyone is for you.
And you are not for everyone.
And that is okay.

76

Have gratitude for all the small things,
while you wait for the big things to arrive.

THIS IS YOUR DAILY REMINDER

There is a past version of you
that is so proud
of how far you've come,
and of the person
you are today.

78

It's okay to question what doesn't feel right.

79

Focus on what you do day to day,
not only the big goal.

80

It's okay to take time to heal
after the hardest moments.

81

So many people love you,
don't focus on those that don't.

82

Be bold in your desires.
They deserve your excitement.

83

You'll be amazed at how things change
when you truly believe in yourself.

Many of your most
wonderful moments are
still on their way.

85

Always treat yourself with the love, kindness, softness, and respect you deserve.

86

It's okay to let go gracefully.
There is beauty in the silence.

87

Be grateful for all that you have.
Be proud of yourself.

88

You have control over your perspective.
You choose your thoughts and your story;
choose wisely.

89

Maybe you are meant to rest right now.
Maybe it's not the time for more, for striving,
or for working exhaustively.

90

Growth is recognising unhealthy habits
and making a change,
no matter how small.

Growth isn't just about moving forward, it's also about letting go, releasing, saying goodbye, and creating space for what's to come.

92

Give yourself permission to wait a little longer
for all that you dream of.

93

It takes great courage to ask for help.

94

Your journey is uniquely yours,
embrace every step.

95

Every small step adds up,
celebrate your progress.

96

Life is forever changing and evolving;
so be gentle, and give yourself permission
to change direction.

97

Perhaps the hardest moments in life
are meant to teach us that
the real magic lies in the little things.

You'll always find magic
if you take a moment to look for it,
often in the most unexpected places.

99

You may not be able to change your past,
but you can choose what you do next.

100

Live for the road trips, the music, the sunshine,
the coffee in your hand, and your bestie beside you.

101

Notice how happy and free you feel,
when you are truly yourself.

102

Craft a life built on love, laughter, happiness, and indulgent luxuries, because life is worth living.

103

You can feel sad or you can feel joyous, often it takes the same amount of energy.

104

There is still time. Time to do all that you dream of and time to become all that you aspire to be.

Notice how sometimes
the biggest worries you carry,
are those that
you have given yourself.

106

Savor the simple things: the smell of fresh coffee,
the warmth of the sun, the thrill of new experiences,
and the love of friends by your side.

107

Keep living for the moments that
make you smile the most.

108

It's okay not to have a set outcome. Often, the best
things come when there are no plans.

109

Give yourself permission to live in your soft era.
No rushing, no hustling. Just being, embracing the
little things, and falling in love with life just as it is.

110

You're the author of your own story.
Create the plot, choose the characters, and
write your own ending

111

Today, choose to stop apologizing for who you are,
and start celebrating it instead.

Never shrink yourself,
to fit into someone else's
version of you.

113

Live life on your own terms,
not by the expectations of others.

114

Your happiness comes first,
never apologize for that.

115

Embrace the messy, imperfect parts,
they're what makes you whole.

116

The people who love you most
will love you for exactly who you are,
not who you pretend to be.

117

When you stop worrying about what others think,
you make room for what *you* think.

118

Be unapologetically yourself,
it's the one thing no one else can be.

THIS IS YOUR DAILY REMINDER

Coffee in hand, glow of the sun,
and a breeze wild and free;
that is my kind of day.

120

Live your life like the sun never sets on your dreams.

121

Life is beautiful in its smallness,
in the quiet moments when you are
simply and boldly yourself.

122

It's all in the little detail; sun-kissed afternoons,
a perfect cup of coffee, and knowing you are exactly
where you're meant to be.

123

Own your moments, big or small.

124

Be the kind of person who sips coffee slowly,
watches the sun rise, and never apologises
for living slowly.

125

Be unapologetically yourself, like a morning sun
that knows it was born to shine.

I've decided to show up
for myself in ways
I never have before.

127

It's time to speak what's on your heart,
even if it makes others uncomfortable.

128

Trust yourself more,
because you know what's best for you.

129

Love the life you are creating,
even if others don't understand it.

130

Don't dim your light just because
it's too bright for someone else.

131

You are your own best storyteller,
don't let the opinions of others write your story.

132

Never make yourself smaller,
to fit into places you have outgrown.

THIS IS YOUR DAILY REMINDER

Don't be afraid
to be different;
be afraid of being
the same as everyone else.

134

It's your life, all the way; so you might as well
enjoy it by simply being yourself.

135

Today, take a little extra time to listen;
you never know what message
your heart may whisper.

136

And maybe your next chapter is about,
building a life you truly love.

137

Maybe you're in a space
where your old self has moved on,
but your newest version hasn't fully arrived yet.

138

How life feels on the inside is what truly matters,
it's never about how it looks from the outside.

139

Let go of the need to control it all.
Instead, embrace the ease and flow of life.

Fall in love with the waiting,
sometimes the best things
take time, and that's okay.
The very best is always
worth waiting for.

141

Your growth is quiet but powerful.
Don't rush it.

142

Celebrate your progress so far this week,
no matter how small.
Every small step matters.

143

Good things take time.
Give yourself the time.

144

You have no idea how amazing
your life will become.

145

Say 'I love you' to those who matter,
and never forget to say it to yourself too.

146

One day you will realise that all you have,
is more than you ever dreamed of.

THIS IS YOUR DAILY REMINDER

Maybe the good days
aren't about luck at all,
but about how you
choose to see them.

148

It's okay to feel disappointed,
even when it was your choice to make.

149

It's okay to make mistakes, choose the wrong path,
or wish to have done things differently.
Just remember that every step has led you to where
you are now, and now is good.

150

Being brave is hard
but the small moments of courage,
always bring something beautifully worthy.

151

The very best days always start
with a beautiful mindset.

152

Be okay with feeling confident, feeling proud
and for being excited about how far you've come.

153

Sometimes, taking a break to rest is exactly
what you need to reset, rejuvenate, and prepare
for what's next.

Stay calm
and allow your mind
to find the answers
you are searching for.

155

You are already prepared for what's next,
even if it doesn't feel that way.
Everything you need is within you.

156

Imagine how far you could be in just twelve months
if you took those first steps today.

157

Maybe your goal is simply to live a life of ease,
going to sleep peacefully and waking up refreshed.
I like that kind of life.

158

Feeling uncomfortable and wanting to give up
yet choosing to stay, that's where the magic happens.

159

Bring the energy that you love to see in others.

160

I love seeing well-loved moments: the gentle
wrinkles on skin, the creases in the pages of a
favourite book, and the softly worn edges of a home.

It's time for a new era.
Time to take that first step,
to love yourself a little more,
to fall in love with the small things.
This is your moment, embrace it
and start to feel the butterflies flutter.

About the Author

Lisa is a writer, dreamer, multi-passionate creator, and mother to two young boys living in Auckland, New Zealand.

Connect with Lisa:
www.lisabuscomb.com
@words_by_wilde_road

Other Books by Lisa Buscomb

Wildly Deserving
Everyday Moments
Lessons & Reminders
Go Where Your Dreams Take You

Available on Amazon, www.lisabuscomb.com,
and wherever good books are sold.